DO YOU HAVE
LEADERSHIP
SKILLS
FOR THE
21ST CENTURY?

RICHARD ANDREW

Evaluate your leadership skills by completing survey questions at the end.

To order additional copies of this book, contact:
Xlibris
844-714-8691
www.Xlibris.com
Orders@Xlibris.com

ISBN: Softcover   979-8-3694-3334-8
       Hardcover   979-8-3694-3335-5
       EBook   979-8-3694-3333-1

Library of Congress Control Number: 2024922894

Print information available on the last page

Rev. date: 11/11/2024

CONTENTS

PREFACE

The purpose of the book is to help individuals and groups to become better leaders in their communities. As a community leader, I can provide key elements that will enhance, motivate, and help achieve successful goals. Readers will learn how to apply their skills and overcome negative obstacles. They will also learn how to sustain long-term leadership goals and learn how to teach leadership to others. Leaders motivate and empower others to become successful.

Leadership changes an individual's behavior and character which will help shape the process of living. This book will provide good results and better leadership skills, which are beneficial in any environment.

DEFINITIONS

Accountability: an obligation or willingness to accept responsibility or to account for one's actions.

Assessing: help to determine initial expectations, ascertain strengths and weaknesses.

Attributes: Characteristics, qualities, or properties that define a person or leader. Attributes of the leader fall into three categories: mental, physical, and emotional.

Authoritarian Leadership: A style of leadership in which the leader tells the employees what needs to be done and how to perform it without getting their advice or ideas.

Beliefs: Assumptions and convictions that a person holds to be true regarding people, concepts, or things.

Brainstorming: A technique for teams that is used to generate ideas on a subject. Each person on the team is asked to think creatively and write down as many ideas as possible.

Building: An activity focused on sustaining and renewing the organization. It involves actions that indicate commitment to the achievement of group or organizational goals.

Character: The sum of an individual's personality traits and the link between a person's values and her behavior.

Communicating: Comprises the ability to express oneself effectively in individual and group situations, either orally or in writing. It involves a sender transmitting an idea to a receiver.

Competency: is behavior-based and describes the individual's characteristics and personality.

Confidence: faith or belief that one will act in a right, proper, or effective way.

Constraint: Any element or factor that prevents a person from reaching a higher lever of performance with respect to her goal.

Collaboration: to work jointly with others or together, especially in an intellectual endeavor.

Culture: The long-term complex phenomenon that can be affected by strategic leaders. Culture represents the shared expectations and self-image of the organization.

Critical Thinking: the process of thinking carefully about a subject or idea, without allowing feelings or opinions to affect you.

Decision-Matrix: A matrix used by teams to evaluate possible solutions to problems.

Decision-Making: The process of reaching logical conclusions, solving problems, analyzing information, and taking appropriate actions based on the conclusions.

Delegative Leadership: A style of leadership in which the leader entrusts decision-making to an employee of a group of employees. The leader is still responsible for their decisions.

Development: The art of developing the competence and confidence of subordinate leaders through role modeling and training and development activities related to their current or future duties.

Direction: guidance or supervision of action or conduct.

Diversity: Committing to establish an environment where the full potential of all employees can be tapped by paying attention to, and taking into account their differences in work background, experience, age, gender, race, ethnic origin, physical abilities, religious belief, sexual orientation, and other perceived differences.

Efficiency: A measure (normally a percentage) of the actual output to the standard output expected.

Empowerment: the act or action of empowering someone or the granting of power, right, or authority to perform various acts or duties.

Enhance: to increase or improve in value, quality, desirability, or attractiveness.

Environment:1. The political, strategic, or operational context within the organization. 2. The external environment is the environment outside the organization.

Ethics: a set of moral principles, a theory or system of moral values in the present day.

Ethos: The spirit (esprit d' corps), moral nature, or guiding beliefs of a community or individual.

Evaluation: Judging the worth, quality, or significance of people, ideas, or things.

Executing: The ability to complete individual and organizational assigned tasks according to specified standards and within certain time criteria or event criteria.

Feedback: The flow of information back to the learner so that actual performance can be compared with planned performance.

Flexibility: The ability of a system to respond quickly, in terms of range and time, to external or internal changes.

Followers: one that follows the opinions or teachings of another.

Goals: the result or achievement toward which effort is directed; aim; end.

Goal Setting: the process of deciding what you want to achieve or what you want someone else to achieve over a particular period.

Horizontal Leadership: Viewing leadership as a system so that information becomes networked. Information now flows horizontally. Differs from tradition leadership in which we view information running vertically or in a hierarchical manner. Also known as flat or vertical leadership.

Human Nature: The common qualities of all human beings.

Improving: A focus on sustaining and renewing the development of individuals and the organization (with a time horizon from months to decades) that requires a need for experimentation and innovation with results that are difficult to quantify. Usually it entails long-term, complex outcomes.

Inclusion: Creating an atmosphere, in which all people feel valued, respected and have the same opportunities as others. Diversity is a range of different people, while inclusion is making them feel welcome and being part of the group.

Influencing: The key feature of leadership, performed through communicating, decision-making, and motivation. A boss tells people what to do, while a leader motivates people by creating a desire within them to accomplish things on their own.

Integrity: A moral virtue that encompasses the sum total of a person's set of values and moral code.

Leaders: a person in control of a group, country, or situation.

Leadership: the set of characteristics that make a good leader.

Leadership Styles: The manner and approach of providing direction, implementing plans, and motivating people.

Learning curve: A curve reflecting the rate of improvement in performing a new task as a learner practices and uses her newly acquired skills.

Learning: An essential shift or progress of the mind where recreation is evident and enjoins activities such as re-engineering, envisioning, changing, adapting, moving into, and creating the future.

Management by Objectives (MBO): A participative goal-setting process that enables the manager or supervisor to construct and communicate the goals of the department to each subordinate.

Mentoring: a person who gives a younger or less experienced person help and advice over time, especially at work or school.

Mindset: a person's way of thinking and their opinions.

Model: A representation of a process or system that shows the most important variables in the system in such a way that analysis of the model leads to insights into the system.

Motivation: enthusiasm for doing something.

Organize: to decide or make arrangements for something to happen.

Organizational behavior: The study and application of knowledge about how people, individuals, and groups act in organizations.

Optimized: to make something as good as possible.

Participative Leadership: A style of leadership in which the leader involves one or more employees in determining what to do and how to do it.

Performance Rating: Observation of a person's performance to rate productivity in terms of a performance standard

Pilot: A pilot plan, product, or system is used to test how good something is before introducing it.

Respect: The regard and recognition of the absolute dignity that every human being possesses. Respect is treating people as they should be treated.

Self-directed work team: A small independent, self-organized, and self-controlling group in which members plan, organize, determine, and manage their duties and actions.

Self-discipline: the ability to make yourself do things you know you should do even when you do not want to.

Skills: an ability to do an activity or job well, especially because you have practiced it.

Spearheaded: to lead something such as an attack or a course of action.

Strategic Planning: a process in which a company's executives decide what they want to achieve and the best actions and use of resources for planning a project.

Supervising: The ability to establish procedures for monitoring and regulating processes, tasks, or activities of employees and their own job, taking actions to monitor the results of delegated tasks or projects.

Tactics: A conceptual action for attaining a particular goal. While strategies are forward-looking, tactical is more or less present or now orientated.

Trait: A distinguishing quality or characteristic of a person. For a trait to be developed in a person, that person must first believe in and value that trait.

Transformational Leadership: a way of bringing big improvements to how an organization operates in which executives persuade managers and employees to work in completely new ways.

Values: Ideas about the worth or importance of things, concepts, and people.

Visioning: Providing a sense of direction for the long term by articulating and defining what has previously remained implicit or unsaid. Visioning often uses images, metaphors, and models that provide a focus for new attention.

INTRODUCTION

Leadership is an ongoing working process and becomes a value to the next generation of leaders. As a leader in the 21st century, we must remember that participation and learning are key elements when leading others. I will give solutions on how to overcome negative obstacles, provide leadership models, and utilize technology for better performance.

The overall goal is to ensure readers that they can lead people, organizations, businesses, students, the work environment, and any other fashion of leadership. The purpose of this project is to provide information about how to succeed and achieve leading roles in life.

Overcoming negative obstacles can help strengthen individual well-being and design new areas for growth. Learning about different leadership strategies can help guide long-term goals.

As a leader, I will include leadership models, financial responsibility tactics, and how to be prepared for new leading objectives. When leading the main goal is to ensure others that you can lead. Having leadership competency will help the process of seeking positive results. My leadership competency helps others become more engaged and motivated. When there is a practice problem, I apply leadership skills that have helped me succeed in other leading roles. Being organized and planned will help develop better competency for achieving goals and problems.

1

HISTORY OF LEADERSHIP

As leaders, the most important value is helping others learn about how to better themselves in their leadership and seek an understanding of what leadership is. However, the history of leadership has developed into many different forms of leadership. Some of the greatest leaders in history have been political, military, and religious men and women.

In history's timeline, we can look back on how leadership was transformed and recognized in the community. Religion helped transform the process of governing society and establishing leaders who uphold order and the law.

The military's rise also increased values for leadership. Thus, creating a foundation that empowers leaders and rulers. Battlefield victories provided leadership acknowledgment and defined how to be a successful leader in any area when leading.

Kings, generals, and religious figures have been the backbone of leadership. Proving order, problem-solving solutions, and cognitive abilities all play a role in shaping society within itself. These individuals influenced the standards for how to be productive in the community, live civilly, and be beneficial to the crown and our community.

In the 19th century, most believed that leaders were born, not made. This theory was considered the Great Man Theory.

It suggested that certain individuals inherited qualities that made them qualified for leadership roles in the community. These individuals had to have the characteristics of intelligence, a natural ability to lead, and desirability. This theory has laid the groundwork for studying what makes a great leader.

"From my own experience and leadership skills, I can positively speak out and say that The Great Man Theory is not true. I grew up in poverty and low-income housing and was raised with no leadership mentors. It was only until my early teens that I began to think and motivate myself to drive my efforts into positive thinking. It was not easy, but over time I strived to seek a leading role in the community that helped me understand how to focus on what makes me a better person. I believe that all theories help with knowing who you are as a leader, and The Great Man Theory shaped my mindset to understand that leaders are made, not born into leadership roles. We must decide who we are as leaders and find individuals that are capable of leading when needed."

However, experts began to question the theory and started to develop other theories, which emerged as trait theories. This specific leadership focused on the personality and characteristics that are associated with leading. It also helps define who is fit to be a good leader. This theory provides a sound rationale for the level of authority. The Great Man Theory was for the citizens and the uncommon wealth of the 19th century. Their leadership style was different but meaningful. It also provided a road map of what is needed to make a society great.

Napoleon Bonaparte and Julius Caesar are two of the most famous examples of this theory. One was a king hero leader, and the other was born into leadership. Both have played a major role in history, which shaped the aspect of leadership. However, anyone can obtain these attributes and qualities to become a great leader. All leaders should follow great examples, but it is our duty to uphold the values and create an opportunity to learn from the mistakes of past leaders.

The Great Man Theory is an excellent example of how to learn and obtain realistic knowledge of what it is to be a great leader. The belief that leaders are born with innate qualities rather than made through experience or education can only state that few leaders exist. However, as we progress, we notice that there are many great leaders who were never born into a leadership role.

2

WHAT'S YOUR LEADING ROLE?

Finding a leading role can be difficult for some, but identifying your leading role can be easy and fun. Some seek sources for leadership, and that helps them define who they are as leaders. However, some don't know where to start, and seeking community involvement is the best solution for beginning a leadership role. Community involvement provides skill sets that can trigger leading identities.

Some leading identities, such as church involvement, policing, food banks, city council, park clean-up, school activities, and any type of volunteer opportunity, will start the process of being a good leader. The most important value is to find something that interests you and/or can help you develop good character skills. Some individuals overthink leadership, are discouraged from leading, or have a bad experience that prevents them from being involved in leading roles.

The prospect of leading is ensuring your followers that you can stay positive and think of solutions that help solve problems. This will increase your ability to understand how to lead effectively. Finding opportunities of interest will help engagement in leading and give a better understanding of why your leadership is important to others.

If you're having trouble seeking leadership opportunities, you should investigate community service clubs, civic boards, county boards, and online media such as Facebook, Craigslist, or Eventbrite. These online sites can help you find local volunteer opportunities that can help develop your leadership skills.

In my personal experience, I have learned that helping others influences me to lead and seek volunteerism. Of course, I started at a young age by helping at school functions, church projects, and city events.

I participated by allowing myself to comprehend the leadership process. Self-discipline was a key element that helped me create a leading role in the community. However, discovering what your interests are will give you a desire to be a good leader and uphold your values.

Seeking great attributes will increase your knowledge and belief that your leadership skills are making a difference. It's best to utilize all opportunities for good leadership and try to understand that you're a tool in a bigger project. Reach your inner self and know what makes you happy. "If you're a good musician, then be the best and inspire others to follow". Be a good example when leading and know that you're helping others in the process.

Evaluating your leadership can also help you define what your leading role is. When effectively utilized within your organization, employment, education, professionalism and other leadership services can be transformative.

This process not only creates opportunities for growth and success but also invites others to step into leading roles. The feedback you provide can be a powerful catalyst for positive change. From formative to diagnostic, summative to ipsative, these methods can help build self-confidence and foster leadership discipline.

I have utilized different evaluations, but the most effective type was self-evaluation and board evaluation, which is a diagnostic method. As Trustees for a Community College, we had annual evaluations that provided us with learning outcomes. This also helped us discover how engaged each member had been and how the Board was progressing. The self-evaluation provided information about how well I was doing as a trustee and how well I was engaged as a member.

Some questions listed on page 5, helped me become more developed, motivated, and skillful for our educational center.

1. **Are you receiving clear and concise background information before**
2. **Board meetings that help you to understand and evaluate Board Agenda items?**
3. **Do you have sufficient access to educational resources outside the Board meetings?**
4. **Have you satisfactorily identified and communicated to management and the Board's informational needs, including appropriate benchmarks to monitor results and identify potential areas of concern regarding performance?**

These types of questions allowed me to understand my role as a community college trustee. Which gave me advance on how to improve or be more productive in the community. The benefits of this evaluation process extend far beyond individual growth. They help me recognize the pivotal role of the Board in serving the students, community, and staff at the college.

Moreover, they provide a platform for growth, improvement, and goal setting while shedding light on areas needing attention. This method fosters accountability and internal feedback, shaping a board to reach its full potential.

One challenge I've seen by other members was completing the evaluation on time. However, finding time to process an assessment can help understand the information correctly. When individuals take time to analyze the evaluation questions, rather than skim reading or rushing through, they can understand how important an evaluation can become.

As leaders, one goal for successful outcomes is to ensure that all challenges can be addressed and resolved before proceeding. Data planning and implementation can have significant value for overall evaluations. Most of the data collected and analyzed will create solutions for better results that can transform how leaders perform or serve their community. While there are potential challenges in self-evaluations such as poor planning, lack of resources, and lack of interest, these can be effectively managed and give meaning to your role in leading.

As future leaders, we can look back on data and seek alternative methods for better outcomes. Researching and understanding what makes good progress in your program evaluation will help keep the process engaging. Seeking your leading role or your purpose is crucial to your leadership. Remember that being and seeking yourself can help you understand what you want out of leadership. Leadership can be as easy as being a manager, directing, upholding values, or giving good advice.

Leadership is not an obligation but a commitment of your own will. All individuals should have an idea of what interest they want to pursue. Finding what makes you happy is the key to authentic leadership. These helping tools within the readings will give you an idea of what type of leadership you want to uphold.

3

LEADERSHIP EQUITY

The most important value of leadership is creating a perspective for all genders and nationalities. Diverse learning can empower, challenge, motivate, and provide positive influence when leading. This chapter will reflect on promoting diversity, inclusion, and equity and how it can change the outcome of the outcome of the leadership system for success.

I will provide support for all those listed above and explain how each one can define a leader.

The purpose of a diverse group will be to help understand how others learn and work together. Thus, creating a rule of character for how individuals act and/or respond to one another. So, whether it's an educational role or a leadership role, diversity can help promote self-awareness, self-confidence, self-esteem, and self-discipline.

First, understanding the difference between diversity, inclusion, and equity will help the learning process for educating others when leading. According to Rosencrance (2021), diversity involves all the way that people are different, including the different characteristics that make one group or individual different from another. Diversity includes race and ethnicity, sexual orientation, socioeconomic status, gender identity, religion, language, and age.

Diversity may also include a range of ideas, perspectives, and values. Equity aims to ensure fair treatment, access, equality of opportunity, and advancement for everyone while also attempting to identify and remove the barriers that have prevented some groups from fully participating.

Equity promotes justice, fairness, and impartiality in systems or institutions' processes, procedures, and resource distribution. When tackling equity, people need to understand the root causes of outcome disparities in society.

Inclusion builds a culture where everyone feels welcome by actively inviting every person or every group to contribute and participate. This inclusive and welcoming environment supports and embraces differences, as well as showing respect to everyone in words and actions.

An inclusive leadership environment is supportive, respectful, and collaborative, aiming to encourage all followers to participate and contribute.

An inclusive leadership environment endeavors to remove all barriers, discrimination, and intolerance. These are all good definitions, providing creativity for engagement and success.

The key is to understand the difference between each benefit and identify its value. Knowing the differences will allow a leader to avoid cultural differences and negative boundaries in a diverse setting.

Recognizing individual differences will allow a leader to focus on developing new skills and tactics for leading in a diverse atmosphere. When leading, it's important to allow time for cultural awareness and learning about different cultures. This will enhance followers' critical thinking skills and provide self-involvement.

Coaching multiculturism when leading will help organize a follower's motivation and/or behavior around other leaders or followers. Embracing your followers in leadership roles will dismantle any barriers that contribute to negative influence. This success will help them develop skills that they can utilize in and out of leading roles.

Teaching diversity to followers and leaders and rooting out bias indicators.

According to diversity and inclusive teaching, Center for Teaching and Assessment of Learning (2022) Teaching diversity, including all learners, and seeking equity is essential for preparing civically engaged adults and creating a society that recognizes the contributions of all people. Teaching diversity entails acknowledging a variety of differences in leadership environments.

Teaching inclusion means embracing difference. Teaching for equity allows the differences to transform the way we think, teach, learn, and act so that all experiences and ways of being are handled with fairness and justice.

These ideas complement each other and enhance leadership opportunities for all to learn when simultaneously engaged. Three imperatives make it essential for us to actively practice teaching for diversity, inclusion, and equity when leading in the community.

Practicing diversity, inclusion, and equity will help followers become more advanced and engage them in higher-level leadership roles.

As a leader, I believe that diversity can help motivate followers and leaders to learn better and understand their identity to become successful individuals.

My knowledge and competency in diversity have given me the skills to become a successful leader. I have also utilized a self-performance rating which helped me understand how to reach higher goals or seek out understanding for large diverse groups. This allows me to understand how to deal with individuals at their level. All leaders should have this ability and know how to react when facing different cultures in a large gathering. As a leader in the community, ethical behavior must provide many aspects of fairness, honesty, leadership, devotion, selflessness, and commitment.

I valued service to others and seek an understanding of how one affects others. This will uphold knowledge of one's character and express feelings for others. All leaders must consider a vision for their followers and create guidelines for social learning and gatherings.

Modeling fairness and respect for others will help enhance the ability of leaders to understand ethical behavior. As the President of a community service club, I uphold all elements that provide positive awareness, which means that I will be an example and provide good ethical character.

Whether respecting the law, respecting the rights of others, taking on responsibility, or upholding leading roles in the community, I must consider how I may affect others. The goal is to provide an environment of welcomeness and safety. I always start the meeting with a cheerful greeting. This allows me to understand how club members are doing and how their day starts. It will enable members to become more open and engaged during the meeting.

Implementing good ethical character will help improve other followers' character of encouragement and well-being. Being able to communicate respectfully helps others create trust of understanding for others. I utilize my educational skills and knowledge to provide good ethical character.

This allows me to help others struggling with negative obstacles and guide them to succeed in an area lacking good ethics. I will always seek positive support to enhance my ability to be a good model and to provide good ethical behavior. I will also implement these elements into the community or any leading role. I aim to educate leaders and followers about good moral character and how to utilize those skills professionally. However, on page 9, a diagram gives a visual aspect of how to lead positively in any diverse environment. It's best to utilize supportive information on how to teach others about diverse competencies.

Diversity Competency

General Characteristics
- Self-awareness, ability to see others' points of view, valuing diverse experiences,
- Recognizing the challenges and complexities of life and willingness to engage them,
- Ability to learn about others' experiences and desire to grow from the knowledge.

The Diversity Competence Model:

Cultural intelligence:

"It is important to learn about cultures that are different from my own."

Diversity Self-Awareness:

"I understand that others may not hold the same ideas and beliefs that I do."

Perspective taking:

"Often I step back from myself and look at the world through the eyes of others to try to understand their point of view."

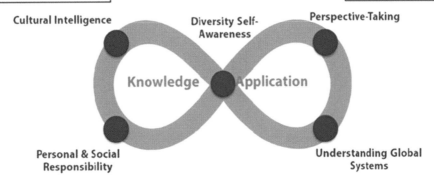

Personal & Social Responsibility:

"I believe I have a certain responsibility to society."

Knowledge Application:

"I can use my knowledge/expertise to address my own experience of diversity."

Understanding Global Systems:

"Historical group conflicts still affect group statuses today."

Research evidence for Diversity Competency

1) **Psychological characteristics**
   High competence related to:
   > Empathy, perspective-taking, collaboration, egalitarianism, self-esteem, guilt, pluralistic orientation and multiculturalism
   Low competence related to:
   > Racial resentment, social dominance, system justification, fear, colorblindness
2) **Behavioral characteristics**
   High competence
   > more likely to have a different race roommate, more diverse experiences in classroom, fewer same race close friends (whites) OR more same race close friends (blacks) learn more from interactions with different people, greater sense of belonging at UD; related to more courses that provide opportunities for intense dialogues.

The mission of the Center for the Study of Diversity (CSD) is to promote academic research and scholarship that facilitate dialogues about and understanding of the social and academic impact of diversity. The Center brings a broadly interdisciplinary focus to its activities, projects, programs, and publications on research and analysis, training, public scholarship, community projects, and information dissemination.

4

AUTHENTIC AND TEAM LEADERSHIP THEORY

In this chapter, I will discuss the values of two types of leadership: authentic and team. These two types of leadership will define a leader's character and how they can empower others to lead. When it comes to leadership, the main goal is to ensure that you can lead at a positive level. These two theories will help develop a good personality and a stronger mentality for leading at national levels and/or in professional settings.

I will discuss the process for each leadership style and give one model that explains team leadership. This chapter will also provide examples of situations within my leadership role and identify how they can be resourceful in my leadership.

Authentic leadership can provide active and motivational development that will build your leadership. However, according to Labrecque (2022), "authentic leadership will focus on transparent and ethical leader behavior and encourage the open sharing of information needed to make decisions while accepting followers "input." The experts seem to agree that authentic leadership is about being yourself and making room for others, too.

It includes a healthy dose of common sense, as well as some ethics thrown in for good measure.

This leadership reflects on values, prioritizing, and organizing to get the maximum benefits when leading. When leading, the authentic leadership model creates energy for those around you, making the environment comfortable to lead. This approach will provide successful outcomes for achieving goals that provide successful results.

In 2003, the theory was developed by Bill George in his book Authentic Leadership, thus creating his model of five distinct qualities that leaders may develop.

The five characteristics are:

1. Passion or purpose provides a sense of knowing how to lead, what to do, and being concerned about how people feel.
2. Behaviors or values that give knowledge of how to perform or function in a professional setting.
3. Relationship/connectedness, which is building a trustworthy foundation that will help the workflow,
4. Self-discipline and consistency will allow for focus, goal setting, and handling difficult situations when they happen.
5. Compassion or heart will help a leader understand when a workload is too heavy for an employee or follower and provide details on how to relieve stress at work or home. Bill's focus is to ensure there is an ethical code for leading.

The strengths of utilizing authentic theory are keeping the team and/or employees engaged and providing satisfaction within the work environment. Being mission-driven will enhance goal setting and create motivation among co-workers and leaders. When leading, acting will help the process for successful input and provide good leadership.

The character's values provide logical reasoning for utilizing the five dimensions. Each one provides principles for being a good leader and knowing how to lead in a confident and beneficial manner. These applications for leadership do apply to today's ongoing leadership and management. Authentic leadership builds character, not style; therefore, this is utilizing a leader's behavior around others and/or how well they can lead. A leader's character will define who they are as a person as well as their strategy for handling difficult situations.

In my own experience as a manager, I have utilized some of these characteristics. For example, when a person needs time off, calls in sick, is unable to perform a task, or has issues with performance, I utilized the genuine heart characteristics that allowed me to help a co-worker. It also provided for relationship building and helped connect the manager and employee to become more effective and motivated to succeed in the job or objective.

The authentic approach will help build a foundation between the manager, employee, leader, and follower. The overall success lies in the leadership and the establishment of effective barriers between individuals. This leadership role is still an ongoing practice and provides good skills for character building.

Another effective theory is team leadership, which is a process that utilizes a group to achieve success and positive performance of an event or professional engagement. Being a leader provides opportunities for growth, and one part of growing is connecting with other leaders to make more of an impact when doing a project or job. Team leadership influences others to give their best and helps build character to reach the highest potential for success.

According to Chicago State University (2022), team leadership must be able to build cohesive and productive work and project teams to achieve the required outputs, either as a work unit or as a component within the organization. Ensures that groups have all the necessary information and explains the reasons for a decision. It Creates the conditions that enable the team to perform at its best (e.g., setting clear direction, providing appropriate structures, and getting the right people). Sets a good example by personally modeling the desired behavior. Expresses positive attitudes and expectations of the team and team members.

Displays willingness to learn from others, including subordinates and peers, and solicits ideas and opinions to help form specific decisions and plans.

These leadership skills will support the team's leadership skills and help them develop how well they work with others. Finding solutions that aid in achieving common goals, tactics, and objectives is crucial.

As a team, a person can rely on a member of the team to help with the transition to successful conclusions. When utilizing team leadership, the main goal is that everyone on the team has input or different strategies for accomplishing goals. This brings enlightenment and enjoyment to the table when leading.

Many people learn from team members and can develop skills that will be helpful when needed. According to McMaster (2013), team leadership theory is not about how a team leads but rather how a leader leads a team. It begins with the leader's mental model, which involves three steps in navigating a problem in the function of the team: identifying the problem, understanding the context, and determining the possibilities.

This leadership helps develop learning skills within the team and allows for an understanding of how each person leads or has different ways of leading. In my own experience, I had the opportunity to utilize team leadership in sports, community service, volunteering, or being employed.

The strength of this leadership is that it helps all members of the team and can create new ideas that help the process of leading.

Both theories can help impact a leader's skills, reputation, and how well they can lead. I have utilized more team leadership in my real-life experiences than authentic theory. When participating in large functions or events, team leadership is more effective and will help with a more successful outcome.

However, I will seek opportunities to utilize the values of the authentic theory. The focus is to learn all about leadership theories so I can know how to handle situations when leading. Being prepared will allow for smooth transitions when leading.

But the important role is to seek other models and styles to become more helpful to other team leaders and/or individuals who are learning about leadership.

As a team leader, there is external support and adequate resources; they are a team, not a group, and have the same vision for outcome, collaboration, and standards of excellence. These are some of the important functions when working as a team. I will continue to seek opportunities to work as a team member and influence others through team leadership.

Below, there is a model of team leadership that gives positive strategies for leading a team.

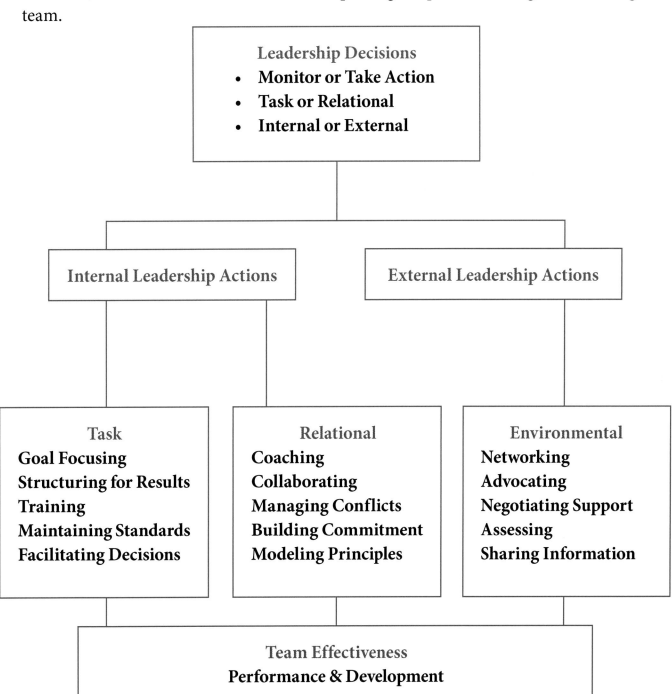

5

LEADERSHIP ETHICS & CODES OF CONDUCT

As a community leader, ethical behavior must include fairness, honesty, leadership, devotion, selflessness, and commitment. I value service to others and seek an understanding of how one affects others. This will uphold knowledge of one's character and express feelings for others. Leaders must consider a vision for the followers that creates guidelines for social learning and safe gatherings. Modeling fairness and respect for others will help enhance the ability of followers and leaders to understand ethical behavior.

As the President of a community service club, I uphold all elements that provide positive awareness, which means that I will be an example and provide good ethical character. Whether respecting the law, respecting the rights of others, taking on responsibility, or upholding leading roles in the community, I must consider how I may affect others. Our goal as leaders is to lead and create an environment of welcomeness and safety. I always start the meeting with a cheerful greeting, not just as a formality but to show that I care about how club members are doing and how their day starts. This simple act can make a significant difference, enabling members to become more open and self-engaged during the meeting.

Implementing good ethical character is not just about personal growth, but about inspiring and improving the character of other followers. Our actions as leaders can serve as a beacon of encouragement and well-being for others, motivating them to strive for the same high standards. Being able to communicate respectfully helps others create trust of understanding for others. I utilize my leadership skills and knowledge to provide good ethical character. This allows me to help others struggling with negative obstacles and guide them to succeed in an area lacking good ethics.

I will always seek positive support to enhance my ability to be a good model and to provide good ethical behavior. I will also implement good moral behavior and use good judgment in the community for any leading role.

I aim to educate followers and leaders about good moral character and how to utilize those skills professionally.

Utilizing the code of ethics can be helpful and give support to how to be a good leader. The code of ethics aims to enrich the values for standards and set rules that provide professionalism and encourage good behavior. Promoting your moral code is always best once an educational establishment has set ethical codes. This allows for recruiting efforts, promotes violation procedures, and ensures the safety of students, the community, and employees. On page 16, there is a list of guidelines and a visual chart for the code of ethics. This is a great example for knowing how to follow the ethos spirit. Below are some bullet points for good ethical behavior.

- Integrity.
- Objectivity.
- Competence.
- Confidentiality.
- Honesty.
- Professionalism.
- Fairness.
- Communication.
- Listing skills

ETHICAL BEHAVIOR

DEFINITION

Ethical behavior refers to actions that align with moral principles and values. It involves making decisions based on fairness, honesty, and respect for others. Ethical behavior transcends legal requirements, focusing on what is right and just. It is a cornerstone of building trust and maintaining integrity in personal and professional relationships.

EXAMPLES

- **Respecting Confidentiality:** A doctor maintaining patient privacy by not disclosing medical information without consent.

- **Fair Treatment:** A manager ensuring equal opportunities for all employees, regardless of race, gender, or background.

HELPFULPROFESSOR.COM

However, these codes of ethics provide organizational skills, team management, and leadership readiness that help set long-term goals. It also is a backbone to the vision and mission of a leadership setting. This provides equal rights for followers and leaders. As a trustee for a community college, the code of ethics allows our board to make decisions that have helped the college move in a positive direction.

These standards help protect employees and students and uphold academic professionalism on and off campus. Having ethical codes gives a good reputation and increases community and education interaction. The code improves accountability and behavior skills.

All leaders should be responsible for speaking out to other leaders and followers when their codes are not enforced. As leaders, we must understand that followers can trust our teaching skills, which allows for understanding and encouragement. This trust is fostered and strengthened by the presence of ethical codes.

These codes help embrace the efforts to teach with respect and guidance. They outline standards for maintaining good relationships with students, parents, employees, city officials, community leaders, and followers, thereby fostering a sense of connection and engagement. Good ethical codes will keep a leader on a safe track for success and progress.

Every leader should seek out opportunities, such as ethical training, code of ethics workshops, and ethical discussions, that will help strengthen the obligations of an educational leader.

Leaders have many ethical codes that help enforce rules and policies that keep institutions, organizations, municipalities, and government agencies operating productively.

These codes support leaders, followers, academics, teachers, administration, and community awareness. I will provide two codes of ethics that I find helpful and can benefit any leadership setting. It helps leaders to analyze the means for right or wrong actions within leadership settings.

It helps to implement more than one code of ethics. My two choices are the Code of Ethical Conduct and the Code of Ethics and Integrity. Both are valued in the leadership field and provide sustainability in educational institutions, non-profits, government, and any other form of agency. They uphold good behavior, creative thinking, judgment, and academic discipline. A model of ethics for leaders will be utilized for higher learning and self-development.

I chose these codes because I have utilized them and found they provide guidelines for creating a foundation for leadership readiness, leadership improvement, and self-discipline. They also help improve how leaders teach and give followers an understanding of what is needed to be successful.

The first-choice Code of Ethical Conduct outlines values and mission, helps establish principles, and defines standards for professionals. It also recommends that leader's models have strong character traits and respect followers with kindness. The moral of this code is to provide good character skills when working with others and support positive outcomes. It respects confidentiality, health, and safety.

If a leader has good ethical codes, they are more likely to be successful in their instruction, personalize learning, increase standard base assessments, and be more active within the community.

This Code of Ethics also informs leaders about what is needed to improve weak areas in a project or objective. Researching ethics can provide a set of principles that guide practices and designs, determining what behaviors are acceptable and how they impact leaders and the community.

"As a trustee, I had the opportunity to help implement this code and seek out research to help our community college conduct itself professionally. This code expresses the values of interactions with students, teachers, parents, and co-workers. It includes responsibility to the profession and helps establish opportunities for educational growth." This code is related to integrity, a key element in Ethical Conduct. Honesty at any level should be followed. It helps build trust among co-workers, teachers, educators, students/parents, organizations, leaders, and the community.

The Code of Ethical Conduct is an umbrella that provides other essential elements that pull together a strong authority that upholds an educational institution's values and mission.

My second choice is the Code of Ethics and Integrity, which outlines the responsibility of a leader. This code helps establish accountability, fairness, respect, and integrity.

This code helps with long-term goals, visions and values, fairness and justice, and leadership. I had the privilege of utilizing this code to help implement new academic programs beneficial to the workforce.

As a board member, we used this ethical code to redirect our vision and seek long-term goals for our college. Starting new certificate programs such as a caterpillar program, heavy equipment operations, policing, and diesel mechanics will help our enrollment and allow for job readiness after completing the program. We utilized data and found that jobs thriving in the community were our opportunity to succeed. We fulfilled our obligations by starting programs that educated students and helped them gain employment in the community.

This code also maintains confidentiality between co-workers and students. It helps fulfill obligations to students and create a useful learning environment on campus.

Both codes of ethics share the same values and uphold the responsibility of educational leaders. They have the exact attributes for creating a learning environment that allows leaders and followers to be themselves in the same setting. These codes prepare leaders for the workforce, community, higher education, and everyday living.

When comparing both codes, they are much alike and give an understanding of the importance of implementing them in business, educational centers, non-profits, or management. The Code of Ethics and Integrity helps with decision-making and establishes standards for behavior among leaders, followers, community, and other working environments. This can help establish a good public image by providing good direction for the outcome of your performance. The Code of Conduct provides a set of rules that help regulate the behavior of employees and students.

As a leader on the board, I have utilized the Code of Conduct to use disciplinary action against employees and students. It also focuses on discrimination, harassment, and conflict of interest. However, both codes are valuable for our educational leadership and should always be utilized. These codes help embrace good behavior skills and allow leaders to learn in a safe environment.

All leaders should follow a model that provides solutions for improving their leadership ability. Having a model can motivate other learners, which will help enforce any code of ethics. Every leader should follow an ethical code that gives them a moral obligation to lead. Seeking help in any area will help advance your skills and provide a shield of protection against those who do not have or follow an ethical code.

We must understand that as leaders, there will be times when some choose not to follow the rules. However, on page 19, a chart outlines a model for being more proactive in improving ethical performance on and off a leadership setting. Being a good leader takes responsibility, actions, and moral values.

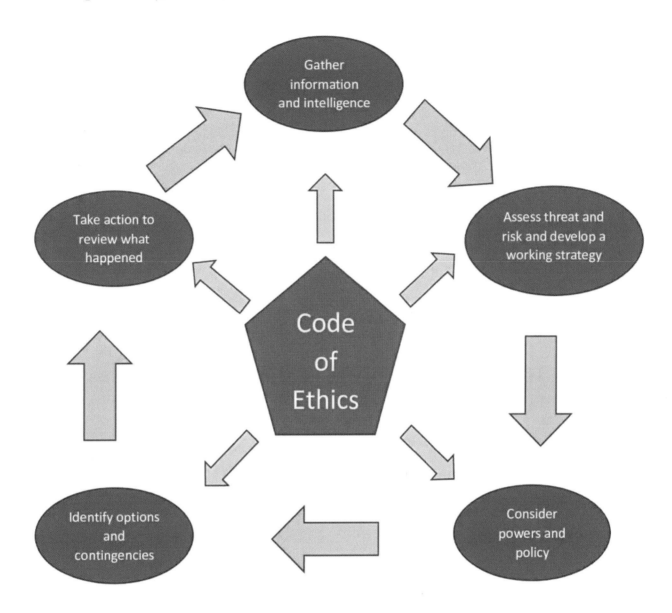

Developing partnerships with community leaders, educational organizations, and stakeholders can help improve and enforce a code of ethics.

Providing a leadership service to the community can be difficult, but implementing ethical codes will help the process and make learning easier. Having ethical training and workshops gives suggestions on how to deal with ongoing issues and will help improve weak areas for improvement.

These codes implement good character skills, which help a leader be more productive and advanced in community service. A leadership setting may only be as positive and productive with these ethical codes. Without them, it would also lack the ability to keep leaders and followers safe. However, understanding why moral codes are vital will help guide the process of implementing them in any leadership setting. Remember to help others who need leadership codes and give them the right opportunity to make a difference when leading. A good leader leads by example. It's important to uphold all ethical codes and follow through with them.

Having the skills and knowledge of good ethical codes will help understand what is needed when faced with a challenge. This will allow you to enforce your knowledge and provide opportunities for positive outcomes. Seeking ethical codes will increase the ability to teach others and find problem-solving solutions for any leader.

6

DIFFERENCE BETWEEN A LEADER AND A MANAGER

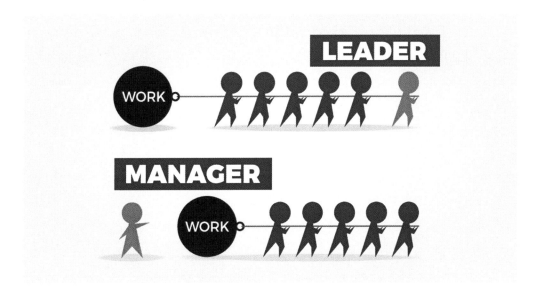

Learning the difference between a leader and a manager will help give a better direction for what type of leadership you uphold. Extreme leaders possess the ability to perform both roles and maintain the skills necessary for each.

However, the managerial culture emphasizes rationality and control. A manager is a problem solver, regardless of whether they focus their energies on goals, resources, organization structures, or people. According to Zaleznik (2024), managers tend to adopt impersonal, if not passive, attitudes toward goals. Managerial goals arise out of necessities rather than desires and, therefore, are deeply embedded in their organization's history and culture. Leaders work in the opposite direction.

Where managers act to limit choices, leaders develop fresh approaches to long-standing problems and open issues to new options. To be effective, leaders must project their ideas onto images that excite people, and only then develop choices that give those images substance. Most managers use some strategic skills to improve the employee work environment. This practice is called "management by objectives," which involves managers and employees working together to set goals and then measuring performance against those goals.

In my opinion, managers are more likely to discipline than teach. A leader's role is to overcome negative situations by teaching them how to solve or fix a problem. Managers expect that everyone will have the same outcome and know how to handle any given situation when needed.

Both roles are similar and provide good tactics for solving problems. Meeting goal objectives, planning, organizing, creativity, and innovation are some skills that drive good managers and leaders. However, most managers utilize the autocratic authoritarian approach. This allows. For more power over others and tend to make choices based on policy or management.

Leaders have a more understanding approach and give more detail in planning. Some leader characteristics are caring about results, showing you "how," giving away credit when things go well, and saying "we." The most important element is empowering others to feel comfortable and welcomed around them.

"Each person accepts one another differently, and as leaders, we have to provide growth for understanding each other." Managers use some strategic skills to improve the employee work environment. This practice is called "management by objectives," which involves managers and employees working together to set goals and then measuring performance against those goals.

However, both have great skills and tactics for leading in many situations they both utilize the same characteristics and learning curves for leading. One example that I have utilized that plays a role in leadership and management is the decision matrix. I have utilized this application as a Trustee for a community college, which helps us make decisions on what areas needed urgent attention, rather than spending time on something that is not so urgent. On page 23 is an example of how to rank and score your concerns:

<u>Decision Matrix</u>

A matrix used by teams to evaluate possible solutions to problems. Each solution is listed. Criteria are selected and listed on the top row to rate the possible solutions. Each possible solution is rated on a numerical scale for each criterion and the rating recorded in the corresponding grid. The ratings of all the criteria for each possible solution are added to determine each solution's score.

The scores are then used to help decide which solution deserves the most attention. This also helps spearhead an objective that some may have difficultly understanding. It helps provide directions of how to complete a goal or vision for your organization.

Example:

Solutions	Criterion 1	Criterion 2	Criterion 3
Hire New Personal	3	4	2
Train workers	5	4	2
Add Computers	5	2	4
Total	13	10	8

This Process can help categorize and priorities your goals and visions. Managers and Leaders do have the same goals, but both are different and can help determine what kind of skills you would like to future. Seeking training in both will help all leading roles. Also remembering that we all have human nature aspects and deserve to be treated the same in any type of environment.

7

UTILIZING TECHNOLOGY WHEN LEADING

In this chapter, I'll express the high demand for digital learning, use of technology and the physical experiences of virtual reality (VR) for leadership purposes. Realism can help influence good ethical behavior and express emotional learning. This effect can help leaders and followers learn to have fun and enhance their ability to be more active.

With technology and research social network skills, a leader can present a unique perspective on successfully integrating ethics, realism, learning, and reality when leading. This approach not only enhances involvement, socialism, individual participation, and productivity but also provides a deeper understanding of virtual reality›s (VR) impact.

Technology empowers leaders and followers to navigate challenges promptly. Today, networking, social media, and other forms of communication mobilize a leader›s performance.

The advantage of technology is that gathering information or data can provide opportunities for growth in a leading role or when achieving significant objectives. Platforms such as Facebook, Zoom, Class Ninja, Meta or other apps can help a leader manage projects and tasks without barriers. Some values to consider below will help understand why technology is essential.

Technology plays a crucial role in problem-solving, enhancing a leader's ability to decipher complicated problems and develop creative solutions. This competence is a vital benefit of technological integration in leadership.

1. Project management: The ability to oversee projects, assign personnel, and achieve deadlines
2. Risk management: The ability to identify and reduce risks related to technological projects
3. Data collection, analysis, and utilization are critical aspects of leadership. Technology enables leaders to ensure that these processes align with ethical and regulatory standards, fostering a sense of responsibility and trustworthiness. Framing, marketing, and communication: The ability to effectively frame, market, and communicate value to various stakeholders

Below is a diagram that gives a visual idea of the value of integrating technology with leadership.

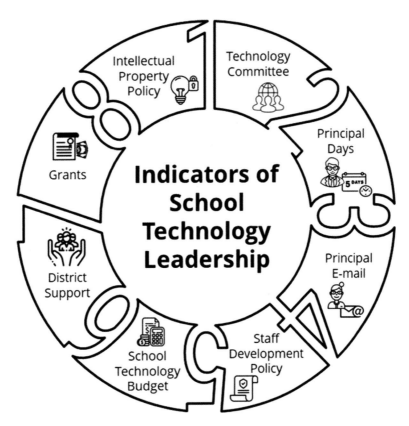

The diagram clearly explains each element affected by technology and leadership. Allowing everyone to learn from technology will help enhance their ability to grow and learn. The effort to take advantage of any technical situations can help all leading roles in the future. As we become more advanced and motivated to drive the economy in a safer environment, technology skills will be more effectively used and adaptive to our lives.

The main goal is to ensure that all leaders and followers can trust that technology will help them be more developed and devoted to reaching their goals. I had the opportunity to grow with technology as a student. My first experience was with a Macintosh computer. It was a learning process, but as I grew, so did my desire to be more educated in all technical aspects. In the 21st century, technology is utilized in every way of life, and we must learn that it's not a necessity but provides advantages for sustainability and successful outcomes.

8

RICHARD'S MODEL FOR SUCCESSFUL OUTCOMES

In my experience trust is a key model that helps identify a leader. Trust is the most important value to obtain. It helps develop a productive relationship with colleagues, the community, parents, leaders, followers, and others who help organizations succeed.

As a trustee for a community college, we utilized this value to the most extent possible. Our mission statement for the college upholds our commitment to students, community, professionalism, and developing academic goals. By building a solid relationship with our admission team, we were able to help students develop training and improve their ability to learn. Being transparent, volunteering, being accountable, and listening to employees and students helped our board find ways to improve its college graduation rate, enrollment and student engagement.

We focused on partnering with community organizations, businesses, political institutions, and job resources, which gave us opportunities for new student development. This allowed for trust, accountability, commitment, student involvement, and long-term relationships. I had the chance to be part of this process, which helped me be more dependable, trustworthy, self-disciplined, and motivated. This allowed me to help uplift students, teachers, and community leaders. It also provides opportunities for seeking higher expectations from college, community leaders, city officials, and academic peers.

Those who lose a trusting relationship with teachers, academic leaders, community superiors or parents must rethink their ability to regain trust. Leaders make mistakes, but considering negative actions can help retain trust. Apologizing is the most helpful tactic and can help correct a problem or even solve an issue.

Rebuilding trust can take time and commitment, which will provide positive feedback. This opportunity can give a perspective on how a leader can grow in their leadership. Active listening and communication will help the rebuilding of a person's trust. Slowing empathy and demonstrating integrity will help the damage of an untrusty person. These skills will help strengthen a person's ability to be trustworthy and give solutions rather than problems. Forgiveness is a step forward and will help leaders understand problems that occur.

We all want successful outcomes when leading. This is where we enjoy hard work, networking, collaboration, and volunteerism for leading. The most important values to understand are what makes a good leader and what you can do to improve your leading role. Creating a learning environment will help the process and give more details of being a good leader. Some of the challenges that some face are how to perform their leadership skills. However, remembering how to control the nervousness, feelings, and negative thoughts will help you overcome obstacles.

Richard's Model for Successful Outcomes

What Makes Great Leaders

Role Modeling
- Inspire
- Be Professional
- Respect One Another
- Lead Positive

Delivering Results
- Assigning Tasks
- Reaching Goals
- Engagement
- Creative Thinking

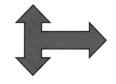

Meet Goals or Vision

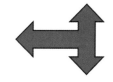

Communication
- Networking
- Verbally or Visual
- Online/Emailing
- Responding/Replying

Accountability
- Trustworthy
- Responsible
- Self-Disciplined
- Willingness

Organized
- Strategic Planning
- Consistent
- Reliable
- Follows Itinerary/Agenda

Embracing Leadership

With this model, any person can follow in the footsteps of a great leader. It takes self-discipline to learn and understand. Having a good character and not letting individuals get the best of you will help your leadership skills. Applying these skills and methods to any leading role will help you succeed and be more motivated.

It's always best to seek help when leading for the first time. Providing opportunities for improvement will create a better experience and give meaningful outcomes. This model is a great example to follow, And I have utilized all areas of leadership. Self-directed work team is a that helps individuals succeed in small groups. It best used to help your self-reflection with in your leadership.

9

THE ROLE OF REFLECTION IN LEADERSHIP

In this chapter, I will discuss the development of reflection leadership and how it can improve results and accomplish goals. The most important value is to ensure that one can lead positively and responsibly.

Self-evaluation and self-direction are the components of reelection leadership, and I will discuss how to apply these skills to gain a better understanding of leadership.

I will also give a list of leadership values and priorities that will help the process achieve successful outcomes.

There will be a reflective step model that gives details for learning from inexperienced or regular leadership opportunities.

I will provide examples of when I utilized reflection in leadership and how it impacted my leadership skills. The most important benefit of leadership is knowing that your self-confidence helps build a foundation for knowledge and understanding. This part of leadership is when the leader reflects on the issues or problems that may arise when leading. Reflection in leadership is what links our performance and gives feedback on how much one can obtain when leading.

According to Neale (2022), self-reflection in leadership means carving out time to review yourself as a leader and is critical for your leadership development. It involves examining your current level of skills, your strengths and weaknesses, your behavioral patterns, and how you seek to influence others. It is also about interrogating your values, goals, and ambitions.

Thus, providing time to seek and acknowledge the mistakes and/or correct any skills that a leader may have. Thinking about the strengths and weaknesses of leadership will improve a leader's role.

However, when reflecting on the experience, it's good to take notes and understand how to redirect leading tactics or skills. The purpose of improving leadership is to contribute to potential outcomes that will help share information with other leaders and/or followers who will lead.

Reflective practice will improve one's ability to focus on the situation at hand. It also helps with the process of leading and learning about new alternative methods for leading successfully. A leader will become more sufficient, responsible, dependable, and disciplined when applying the role of reflection in leadership development.

When becoming a great leader, one must reflect on their mistakes and know how to overcome them.

The model on page 32 outlines a five-step cycle for responding to a situation. According to Gibbs (2022), many people learn best from experience. However, they cannot learn anything if they don't reflect on their knowledge and consciously think about how they could do better next time.

The model supports the motivation and effort needed to lead positively. It gives leaders and followers guidelines that can keep them on track for seeking out resources and creating a boundary to succeed. This model is simple and should be used in any leading role. It also helps to understand the values of learning and teaching leadership. See model for more visual understanding.

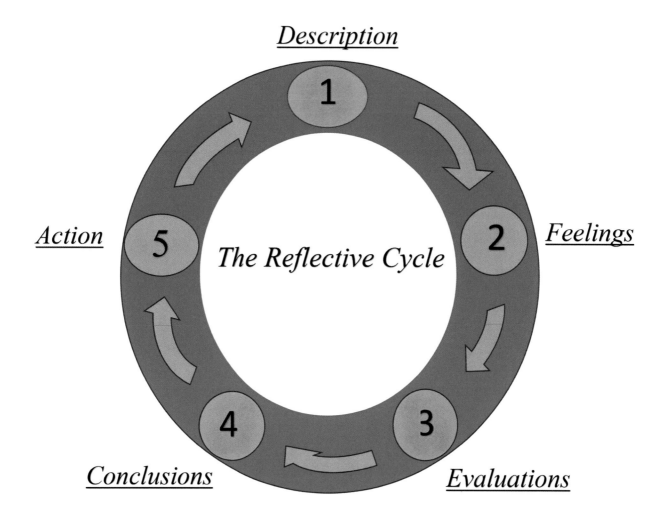

The steps provide how to filter the negative feedback, rethink the situation, and move forward positively. In the readings of reflective leadership practice for the academic chair, I utilized all leadership values and found that discipline, integrity, honesty, accountability, and empowerment are my top five values for leading.

The reflective cycle helps motivate and define leaders. Discipline is a value that aids in focusing on the goal and reducing stress. Being self-disciplined will help a leader understand the workload and acknowledge the hardships of leading. The second value is integrity, which enables a leader to lead through their actions. It also projects a leader's performance and builds credibility on their actions.

Honesty provides the values of truthfulness and commitment. When leading, those that you lead must trust you, and honesty helps build a foundation for understanding one another. This value will also allow a leader to reflect on their leadership skills and how they lead. Being honest with yourself will allow you to learn from your mistakes, rather than not being honest and not leading positively.

Accountability is a value that all leaders must have. This value is key to leading; one can't be a leader if they are not able to commit. Accountable leaders communicate and follow through with goals and objectives.

Empowerment is the last value I use for successful leadership. This allows a leader to be self-confident and self-sufficient when leading. When leading, delegating helps the chain of command. This allows the leader to direct with authority and give direction when making decisions.

When leading, my top five priorities are:

1. **Visioning,** which is a key factor in my leadership, allows me to set long or short-term goals and achieve them by acting on them.

    Having a vision when leading will foster a structure for followers who seek guidance, thus providing a successful outcome to the vision.

2. **Mastery** can become a skill for long-term leadership, and it provides, reflection, and practice, inspires others, and resolves conflicts. This type of leadership takes time and trial but can be accomplished with hard work and understanding.

3. **Networking** will help a leader become more advanced and skillful in the role. This is an opportunity for growth and communication. A leader can obtain higher knowledge of how to lead when networking with other leaders.

4. **Influencing** will help motivation and team success. This type of leadership provides an impact on others and shows how well a person can lead. Being a positive influence will increase your leadership results.

5. **Personal Development** is a style that gives self-awareness, a positive image, acknowledgment of behavior, and personal reflection on leading. I will continue to learn how to become a better master leader by learning, researching, understanding, and seeking opportunities to lead others. The role of reflection is that leadership should give positive results and provide feedback. This support can help build and strengthen a leader's self-image. All leaders can seek self-image and self-awareness of their performance and what they need to improve. Creating an opportunity to seek self-reflection will enhance their ability to teach others and direct those who need good leadership skills.

This is a learning process and experience that makes a difference. Everyone can achieve the ability to understand how to gain good results and how to make a difference in someone's life. Seeking integrity, commitment, and self-discipline is the key to being a great leader.

10

ETHICAL DECISION-MAKING FRAMEWORK

As leaders there is a value of ethics and theory that help distribute information on how to obtain skills and enhance their ability to be great leaders.

In this chapter I will describe Fisher's article on the six-step model for ethical decision making.

This will include nine sequel questions that help understand ethical decision making. There will be a chart that will give an easier understanding of the importance of ethical values and theory practice. I will give personal experience of when the six-step application was effective when leading.

Having good ethical practice will help your leadership be more devoted to understanding how to apply the skills in the work force, community, education, municipals and within organizations. The code of ethics aims to enrich the values for standards and set rules that provide professionalism and encourage good behavior.

This allows for recruiting efforts, promotes violation procedures, and ensures the safety of students, the community, and employees. These six steps will help provide actions as a leader and give solutions for challenges or obstacles that may happen.

They are listed:

- **Step 1: Identification of the ethical problem**
- **Step 2: Identify the relevant ethical principles, standards, guidelines**
- **Step 3: Identify the relevant laws, regulations, and policies**
- **Step 4: Understand stakeholder perspectives**
- **Step 5: Consider alternatives and developing and implementing a plan**
- **Step 6: Monitor and evaluate the plan**

Leaders must uphold this framework of ethics, which will allow for more positive results and provide an understanding of what a good leader is.

In my own experience, I utilized this framework that helped me be more developed in decision-making and how to evaluate a situation.

For example, as a legal and educational consultant, I had to recognize an ethical issue, get the facts, and evaluate alternative actions for all my clients. I would seek out unethical concerns and help develop a plan for success or regain stability. Reaching out to stakeholders, community organizations, and educational resources helped my clients reach their goals.

I used Fisher's six steps to help guide me through this process and understand the importance of following through with the steps. I helped my clients achieve higher education, community involvement, and overcome challenges. However, the model on page 36 best describes how to make ethical decisions. The visual helps ensure that leading isn't tricky but fun when you join forces to make a difference. The outcomes can be challenging but collaborating and seeking help when making decisions can make or break your leadership skills.

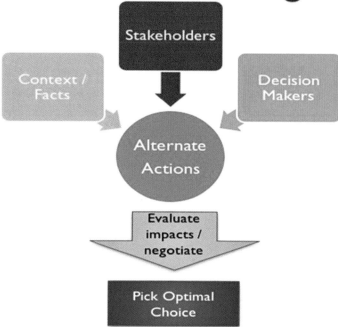

Ethical Decision Making Model

Promoting your moral code is always best once an educational establishment has set ethical codes.

The six-step model is informed by nine sequential questions that help the process of decision making. They are as follows:

1. **What is the issue?**
2. **Why is a decision needed?**
3. **What are the alternatives?**
4. **What are the potential consequences of each alternative?**
5. **How likely or unlikely and valuable or adverse is each consequence?**
6. **Does each alternative comply with laws, polices, and standards of conduct?**
7. **What are the ethical considerations in each alternative and consequences?**
8. **What is the decision.**
9. **Was the decision effective?**

These questions help make decisions; they also help provide understanding and not make rational decisions. All the above methods can help leaders be more prepared and developed for making decisions. Gathering all the facts and providing honest and fair judgment is essential. Fisher's models should be utilized in all areas of leading.

Learning to make good decisions can encourage others to find alternatives for punishment. The findings have influenced me to know how to make crucial decisions and understand why I made them. As a Trustee for a community college, I've made decisions that significantly impact on the college, the county, students, the community, and employees. This understanding has always motivated me to conduct thorough research and develop resources before voting on significant issues.

Leaders must take their time and evaluate problems. This approach, rather than relying on instinct, ensures that the right decision is made for everyone. Fisher's model helps identify what a leader should be. It also gives excellent qualities in how to achieve those skills. It's always best to reach out to resources that provide detailed examples of ethical behavior. Seeking outside sources such as non-profits, donors, educational centers, churches, and other organizations that have upheld standards for ethical behavior can help in that process. However, as a leader, I have had the opportunity to be a part of an ongoing ethical situation.

Having an established team of administrators helped me make changes within the school to make social justice more accessible, understandable, and knowledgeable to all students and employees.

The school board and the principal of an academic center usually decides this team. In my situation at the college level, we had academic administrators oversee the problems of ongoing issues with social justice. This branch of administrators would also seek out groups or individuals that could help improve our social justice environment on and off campus. However, this team's objective was to create more fair and equal opportunities for all diverse students. They also provided equal access to resources, economic benefits, political influences, and social awareness.

Creating a welcoming social justice environment can improve the quality of life in healthcare, educational learning, living environment, parenting skills, and community engagement.

Having a team will help leaders be more prepared for challenges. Community stakeholders are the most valuable resources for all leaders. It will help them discover opportunities to be active in their endowment, employment, community, or living area. Building relationships with these community stakeholders can solve ongoing issues that some leaders need help to face. Another example of a community stakeholder I was involved in was the city transit department. Some of our students lived in areas with no city bus routes. Our college partnered with the city bus transportation department to help gain access to assist students in attending our college.

The partnership included free student bus passes, paid for by the college. Our college also gained advertising on bus benches, buses, and bus stop stations. The partnership allowed us to increase our student enrollment, which also helped students be more active in learning.

Providing access to all leaders is a form of achieving social justice. Other community stakeholders significantly impacting leaders are:

- Job resource centers.
- The Chamber of Commerce.
- The City Mayor's office.
- Education resources.
- The Police and Fire Department
- Medical Hospitals.
- Community Advocates.

These are some of the stakeholders who contribute to ongoing ethical issues and decision-making. As listed above, people employed by local organizations can help build relationships with leaders and provide valuable information for succeeding in their community.

Most of these community stakeholders can bring in revenue and opportunities to help break barriers at the leadership level. Creating equal rights and accessibility to all individuals can help leaders operate to their maximum potential. Leaders should contact community officials to encourage others to engage in all leading activities.

This example helps make an educational center more accessible and builds trusting relationships with all stakeholders involved in education. Leaders must create a foundation with all diverse students to help implement the fundamental learning skills required to succeed in any setting. An active leader helps followers be more productive in leading settings and provides self-discipline and learning opportunities.

These essential experiences helped me understand the problem and make a clear decision that would impact the community. I enjoyed working with the stakeholders and administration to make our college a better place for diverse individuals.

11

TRANSFORMATION LEADERSHIP

In this chapter, I will discuss the importance of transformational leadership and the strengths and weaknesses of utilizing this style. A good leader will know how to utilize this style when changing roles while leading. I will also provide examples of my own experience and how it affected my leadership role.

This style helps a leader become more developed and knowledgeable about how to handle difficult situations.

I will provide a model example of the four elements, which will help explain the steps for transformational leadership. Transformational leadership helps inspire, seek self-interest, set clear goals, meet high expectations, and provide support to other leaders or followers.

According to Cherry (2022), transformational leadership is a leadership style that can inspire positive changes in those who follow. Transformational leaders are generally energetic, enthusiastic, and passionate. Not only are these leaders concerned and involved in the process, but they are also focused on helping every member of the group succeed as well.

This type of leadership helps others become motivated and centered on overcoming negative obstacles. Being a trust-based leader will help the success of other leaders and/or followers.

When helping others succeed, the objective or project becomes more achievable. This style will help with vision-seeking and/or fulfilling the long- or short-term vision. Transformational leadership facilitates the processes of managing, coaching, understanding, and motivating, as well as the message of leading positively.

Transformational leadership is vision-based and helps unite other leaders to be involved and stay focused on the objective. The advantage of this style is that team motivation, building strong relationships, and encouraging collaboration give team members autonomy to do their jobs and can lead to more creativity, growth, and empathy in teams. Below is a list of the four components that support transformational leadership.

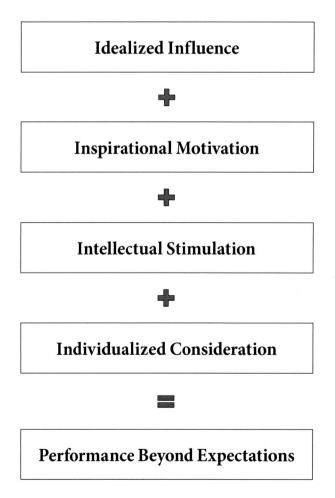

This element helps develop good skills for leading and teaching others about transformational leadership. The goal of leadership is to ensure that they are doing a good job. Having the knowledge and skills will help them adapt and become skilled when leading.

This type of leadership is applied at professional levels or when leading large groups. When leading an organization or corporation, this type of leadership will be most beneficial. It helps for growth, builds communication skills and collaboration, and creates more participation from employees and/or followers. However, some disadvantages are that it does not work well with a strong vision setting and can result in risk-taking.

I believe that the effectiveness of this style largely depends on how you apply it. Each element can help resolve any obstacle and create an understanding of how to approach a situation when needed.

Some of our great leaders, such as Abraham Lincoln, Martin Luther King Jr., Indra Nooyi, and Margaret Thatcher, are good examples of those who utilized transformational leadership. I have utilized this style and had great success.

In my experience of leadership, the transformational style helped me become faster and more dependable, accomplish goals and visions, create self-interest, and reach high expectations. I had the opportunity to lead a team of fifty for a yearly Christian concert that was highly demanding and required the support and encouragement of others. I participated as a security officer for a musical concert. My job was to lead the team in crowd control, stage management, and backstage management. Leading a group of fifty was not difficult, but it took self-discipline, motivation, team vision, participation, and organization.

I exceeded my leadership skills and helped others succeed and become more developed in their role as leaders. According to DiFranza (2022), at the most basic level, transformational leadership is used to inspire employees to look ahead with a focus on the greater good and to function as a single unit with a common goal in mind. It is not until a leader can accomplish these steps that a successful transformation can begin.

This leadership style has helped me become responsible and self-dependable. I've had great experience with larger groups when leading. When leading larger groups, it helps me understand how to be ready for the unexpected and how to handle situations that occur when leading. In this paper, I have learned that anyone can apply transformational skills to their leadership. This style will help others become successful and motivated to lead larger groups or teams.

My communication skills, motivation, goal setting, self-engagement, and critical thinking skills have been influenced to continue to find opportunities to lead. The main objective is to ensure that you can lead at high volume and seek high expectations that will benefit your ability to lead and/or teach about transformational leadership. This process can help in many ways, but knowing how to utilize your skills at any given time will help you succeed at all costs.

Seeking help in all areas will enhance your ability to accept major leading roles and give you more experience. The leader aims to provide safety and accountability which ensures your followers you have what it takes to be a leader. Maintaining leadership morals and evaluating situations can help your skills improve and elevate your ability to overcome any obstacle. Finding alternatives for leading directly is a great way to utilize transformational skills.

12

FINANCIAL LEADERSHIP

As leaders, we must appreciate the value of fundraising, budgeting, annual financial obligations, and keeping track of all financial records. Money plays a vital role in leadership and can define a leader's dependability for honesty.

Some of the roles a leader may consider are allocating funds, exploring fundraising opportunities, managing cash flow, establishing a bank account, and buying goods for annual events or projects.

Some key traits of financial leaders include adaptability, integrity, and continued learning. Some leaders will have an educational degree in finance. However, this type of leadership does not mean you need an academic degree.

Anyone can learn in the decision-making process for money. To achieve good outcomes in your leadership, developing good money practices can help build your skills for accepting more prominent leading roles.

Being effective in every leading area can provide significant growth and learning opportunities. Some of the most outstanding businessmen and women are financial leaders. This type of leadership will help define your interest in keeping money, negotiating, dealing with annual tax preparations, and any other obligation for having a budget. It's best to understand the basics of financial duties, such as keeping track of sales during a bake sale or having your raffles permit for an event or drawing.

Knowing the state and federal guidelines when dealing with money will help your leadership skills develop.

This can be easy and informative. However, creating an opportunity to learn this type of leadership will help you build relationships with other organizations, city managers, education administrators, and other leaders who deal with financial obligations annually. This can also help you advance to higher-paid positions and deal with finances.

Below there will be a visual model that gives you a better understanding of how to obtain good financial leadership skills. This visual will help enhance your ability to know what is needed to seek out success and proceed with responsible actions.

All the elements below will give you a better understanding of how to deal with money and what is helpful as a leader. This process can provide excellent outcomes that will help you fulfill any obligations for dealing with money. Seeking these elements will ensure the safety and trust of a leader.

Author: Harish Maheshwari

An ethical understanding of how to lead in finances will help with the budgeting and goal-reaching process. Spending wisely, creating adequate records, and managing time will help improve the overall control of the funds. Also, ensuring this role is fulfilled by a person of good trust and integrity is essential. For example: "I would not ask a person with a criminal record of stealing or the desire to spend funds for their gain to hold a position dealing with money" This leadership position is critical and will significantly impact all those involved.

"I'm sure that we all hear stories and know about those who misuse their leadership role to gain profit for their interests". This is essential to leading and should not be taken advantage of. In my own experience, I have witnessed many times that individuals misuse funds and or direct funds for their gain. This type of malpractice is a crime and should be committed by those who misuse funds in any leading role.

The most important value to rely on is taking the initiative to make the right choices and be a good leader. Taking advantage of people is not a leader's characteristic. Trying to make a difference and knowing right from wrong will ensure that other leaders and followers can trust you. It's important to value the effort to handle money or funds in a manner that is allocated to its appropriate place. Optimizing your situations when dealing with money will give logical reasoning for spending.

13

THINK BIG

Thinking outside the classroom provides educators and leaders with growth and academic achievement opportunities. Having the fundamental image of creating big goals and dreams can help an individual be successful at any level.

I will discuss how to unlock the secrets of thinking differently and thinking big when advancing in education and leadership. I will include details of how to reach higher goals and be more productive in achieving success. Reading, researching and taking lead have taught me how to think about bigger goals and think differently or creatively to seek more significant outcomes.

Thinking outside an objective can help productivity and motivation and give good feedback for reaching your goals.

Long-term goals can help the impact of a bigger goal and support your leadership. "Steve Jobs was my life". Mr. Jobs was a person who thought differently and was thinking big.

His big vision was to enhance the computer industry and improve communication, network, technology and advancement in daily living. His big goals and dreams, faced challenges, but he continued to be motivated and self-inspired to overcome all negative obstacles.

As of now, Mr. Jobs' vision has grown bigger and has impacted many individuals worldwide.

Thinking big or differently can significantly enhance your leadership skills and learning ability. It's important to recognize that when tackling a large project or leading a large group, your skills will be honed as you learn to navigate and respond to game-changing situations.

This process creates a valuable learning curve for future projects or leadership roles.

When undertaking significant objectives, it's crucial to identify unique propositions. What sets your project apart? What unique value can your project offer? How did your startup begin?

These are some of the questions that one may ask them self, when beginning a big project. The startup phase is where the details of a big project come to life, allowing you to execute your vision for your goals.

Success in thinking big can open growth opportunities and inspire others to join your vision. Taking risks and believing in yourself will guide your objective and inspire new ideas for better solutions. Setting ambitious goals will test your motivation and drive you to solve ongoing problems.

When you embark on an ambitious goal-setting journey, you will likely encounter a set of common challenges. These include:

1. Access to capital. Securing adequate capital is one of the most significant hurdles you may face when thinking big for your startup. With the necessary funding, launching your project can be a manageable task.
2. Managing growth. Once your business starts to grow, you'll need to be able to manage that growth effectively. This can be a challenge, but it's essential to ensure that your business can scale.
3. Making sacrifices. When starting a business, you may have to make some sacrifices. You may need to work long hours or make personal sacrifices to make your business successful.

These are just a few challenges you may face when thinking big for your startup. However, if you're prepared for them and have a solid plan, you can overcome them and succeed. These challenges are the most important and will allow you to be well-prepared for your big project.

Belief in oneself is the cornerstone of thinking big or differently.

This belief not only provides motivation and understanding for achieving higher expectations but also enhances your ability to lead and educate others about taking on significant tasks or projects. A focused mindset will enable you to identify and overcome the obstacles in your big project, turning them into opportunities for growth and success.

Below are elements that give an understanding of how to stay on track for reaching your big goals or projects.

1. **Thought Paralysis:** Our actions reflect our thoughts, shaping the course of our lives. Many of us confine our thinking, limiting the direction of our thoughts, which in turn leads to a paralysis of our actions. We settle for small victories, branding ourselves as failures for not reaching the pinnacle of success. But remember, this is not the end. There is always potential for growth and change.

2. **Fear of criticism:** What will people think about me when discussing something extraordinary? A general question comes to mind and is the fear of being criticized. What will happen if they fail to achieve what they had set out for? It stops the majority from talking about something big and extraordinary.

3. **Believe in scarcity:** Every person has different potential and competencies; however, a few people have the potential and capabilities but need to use them. They tend to believe that since they belong to an environment of non-achievers, they cannot achieve anything. People underestimate themselves and do not believe in their potential. This puts a full stop to their belief system, and they remain away from their Real Wants.

4. **Luck dominance:** A human mind always receives what it observes from society. When a person sees a luxury car passing by, sees a big house, meets some positive personalities, or any positive relations, they create positive feelings for all those. If others can achieve and live their dreams, we can do it; I can also live my dream.

These people observe, feel, learn, and act to achieve their dreams. They stop being in the mediocre class and start thinking big to achieve big. Some people think negatively; to them, another's success seems like an act of luck rather than the result of determination, hard work, and positive thinking. It's luck that dominates in any success story.

These four elements will help identify your ability to handle big goals and justify following through with an objective. They also provide information on being successful, self-motivated, thinking differently, and creating big visions or goals as educators and leaders. Creating big visions has bidirectional impacts and will give followers inspiration to help and want to learn about being a leader or join in on big projects.

In my own experience I have been part of many big projects, in which it helps build my leadership skills and gives me an understanding of to take on big projects.

During my 4th year of college, I took on a significant, leading role in the community. As a student working on my bachelor's in legal studies, I found myself engaging in the community by volunteering, sitting on committees, and joining service clubs. These actions helped me understand the need to uphold self-esteem, motivation, and positive awareness.

Thinking differently helped me underline how to obtain higher learning and become successful in any area. I knew I had to think big or stop all ongoing commitments as a campus leader and community leader. So, I decided to run for an elected position within my district. I knew that I was facing significant challenges and different aspects of life. However, with my motivation and desire to help students and county residents, I elected to run for a trustee position at a community college.

This was a significant obligation, considering I was still in school and only had a few years of experience on boards and commissions.

I followed my goal and started campaigning for the upcoming election in 2014. There were obstacles and negative feedback. Some spoke out loud about my desire to run for office and felt that I was too young or needed to gain experience at the county level. However, with dedication and leadership, I won my first election and served as Trustee for San Joaquin Delta College. I was overwhelmed and excited to take on the role of Trustee.

I also help motivate students and other educators to become more productive and devoted to campus activities. Within my first term, I helped create a five-year master plan and provided our college with a new program that increased student enrollment and enhanced community engagement.

Thinking big or differently is an action word, which can be empowered by one's outcome if they choose to follow through. I knew that deciding to run for an elected office would be challenging and difficult, but thinking differently helped me understand how to reach my goals and gave me an opportunity to succeed at a big level.

I have learned that the following steps for achieving big goals can help anyone understand the challenges and opportunities that will have a major impact on any big goal or project. Thinking differently, Thinking Big inspired me to challenge myself to reach bigger goals or projects. When reaching bigger goals, we can provide positive leadership skills and educate others how to reach their bigger goals in life. Whether it's working hard to hold a major event or fulfilling a goal, we should be motivated to share the elements of reaching such goals.

Creating a learning environment for others will help them become more advanced and prepared to think differently or big. Thinking big will always provide significant results. Knowing that you can make a difference on a large scale will provide opportunities for leadership growth and give you an understanding of how to tackle big dreams.

Being successful is a great feeling that everyone should experience, but not all will endeavor to achieve it because they lack the thought of not thinking big. It's essential not to crush a person's dream and try to be the best influence possible. Being a great leader will always help make a difference.

14

SAD FORMULA

In this chapter, I will continue to discuss how to make sound ethical decisions and what is needed to improve one's ability to express good ethical behavior. I will provide a formula that explains integrating elements of critical thinking with moral reasoning.

I will also include bullet points that give a better understanding of how to achieve good ethical character and achieve success when leading.

Understanding and considering alternative frameworks is crucial for a leader's growth and preparedness to take on challenging roles. This framework is particularly useful in resolving ambiguous situations. Similarly, utilitarianism can be a valuable tool in organizations or teams when dealing with complex situations that involve trade-offs, uncertainties, and multiple stakeholders.

This formula helps individuals make critical decisions based on principles, values, consideration of factors, and examination. By including all elements, a leader can make clear decisions without making any mistakes.

As a leader, making the right decisions for followers, the community, stakeholders, and other organizational resources is essential. However, there is a formula that helps clarify ethical development and implement critical thinking.

The SAD formula is a framework that identifies the facts of a problem and seeks out sufficient information to understand how to solve it without a dilemma. This approach helps build character and self-awareness for others. Listed below is the SAD Formula

- Situation Definition
  - ✓ Description of Facts
  - ✓ Identification of principles
  - ✓ Statement of ethical issue or question
- Analysis
  - ✓ Weighing of competing principles and values
  - ✓ Consideration of external factors
  - ✓ Examination of duties to various parties
  - ✓ Discussion of applicable ethical theories
- Decision
  - ✓ Rendering of moral agents' decision
  - ✓ Defense of that decision based on moral theory

As leaders, we can consider those we lead and how they affect others. Leaders can effectively address problems by applying critical thinking and reasoning.

Critical thinking, a rational approach that emphasizes careful analysis and evaluation, is key to making decisions.

It involves defining the problem and evaluating the solutions adopted. The SAD Formula is a powerful tool for making clear, ethical decisions.

It guides individuals to consider principles, values, and factors, and to conduct a thorough examination.

By incorporating all three elements, a leader can confidently make decisions without the risk of errors. As a leader, it's crucial to make the right decisions for followers, the community, stakeholders, and other educational resources. Critical thinking gives more detail of a solution and provides facts about how to handle such acts.

This framework for ethical principles allows for everyone to know what actions have taken place and what is needed to make right choices by leaders and educators.

I have utilized this approach as a Trustee for a community college; it helped me make decisions that affected the students, community, employees, and parents.

It allowed me to make good decisions not based on instinct, pressure, or outside influences.

Whether it was starting a program, seeking new partnerships, or seeking funding for events, this approach helped me understand the value of analysis, critical thinking, and identifying ethical issues. This Formula helped me understand the importance of receiving all the facts and seeking out the elements before making a crucial decision.

Solving dilemmas at a college level was ongoing, and my choices affected many students, the community, and parents. This learning approach can help increase the ability to understand how to make decisions.

It will provide reasonable thinking and honesty that can help make financial decisions for an individual.

I have utilized this Formula, which helped me understand how to analyze problems and make clear decisions without internal influences. It will provide reasonable thinking and honesty that can help make financial decisions for an individual.

The formula should be utilized to help you create better environments for others and give you an understanding of how to improve in leading roles. This practice is ongoing and can create opportunities that streamline your vision for any type of industry. Following this formula will ensure self-discipline and motivate others to be creative.

15

MY LEADERSHIP EXPERIENCE

Some of my best efforts when leading others are to make sure that the group setting is positive, safe, and motivational. However, recently I had the opportunity to participate in the Oregan 22 Track & Field World Athletic Championships. For this event, they hired me as a security supervisor, where I managed a team of 15 security officers.

The setting was more than what I expected, and I knew that delegating skills, goal setting, authoritarian skills, and participative skills were resourceful for a positive outcome.

My position was to supervise a team that controlled one side of the event entrance. We ensured the screening and identification of all participants and ticket holders prior to their entry. I knew that to control a team of 15, I needed to delegate each person to the importance of crowd control and safety, customer curiosity, performing inspections and bag checking, guarding checkpoints, and daily routine operations for securing an entrance. Each style helped me constructively navigate the group.

The two styles I reflected on the most were authoritarian skills and participative skills. Authoritarian skills help me distribute the information in a manner that each person will understand. I was responsible for the group, and creating a line between us allowed me to create pathways for the group to become self-disciplined in their role as security officers. This leadership style helped develop a professional identity for the group that inspired self-confidence, reliability, organizational skills, and higher standards for success.

As I reflect on the event's success, I would not change anything. These styles helped me identify how to approach each team member.

Participative skills allowed me to interact with and assist each person in the group. It also helped build relationship skills, feedback, and self-awareness of how to lead. This style is good for communication, trust, goal achievement, and group satisfaction. I used this skill to help motivate and encourage the team to achieve greater success.

I believe that my approach was a successful one. The group delivered with high expectations and provided excellent service to the event's outcome. My approach allowed me to understand each person at a personal level and know what weak areas needed improvement. This allowed me to understand how to interact with my followers.

Over 4 weeks, I learned how to guide, lead, motivate, and create better individuals for future professional experiences. My practices during this time have taught me to understand that not all people learn the same and some individuals have a hard time understanding. The important value is to know how to speak, listen, and relay information.

Proving good communication skills will always allow good problem-solving, which will help you succeed in any situation that you may face. Trying to be a good leader will sometimes work in your favor. But knowing that you stay respectful and positive will ensure your safety and keep your leadership reputation in good standing. With all my experiences, I have utilized all these models, practices, and elements to help me be successful when leading. It's important to seek out what you're good at and follow through. Many have a talent for being great leaders but fail to understand the process. So, whether it's leading a group, school activity, community event, or employment position, your role is important, and such actions will be accounted for.

The best knowledge and understanding of leading can make you a better leader. Uphold all values and respect others as you would like to be respected. I enjoy leading and following; it has significantly impacted my life.

16

CONCLUSION

"Check mate". But the game is not over yet. Throughout my writings, I became interested in learning more about what makes a great leader. This practice and discovery helped me understand that I want to learn more about leadership. However, my script's material will help you be a better person and leader. You have contributed significantly to how you impact others around you and within your community. These leadership passages will help you navigate your path to righteousness and understanding.

I know that your talents and motivation will suit you well. Please be mindful of how you lead and consider that some individuals need our help to be successful in life. With all my leadership experience, I would only have it knowing that I also need help. We can all make a difference in someone's life and help those needing good leadership practices. These models and examples have helped me become an achiever and gave me a light at the end of the tunnel. So, whether you're a teacher, coach, police officer, businessman, volunteer, or any other leading role in your community, you have impacted lives.

Serving as a leader and a follower has been a pleasure, but more leading roles still need fulfillment. Remember that you're not alone and make every leading role count. Give yourself applause and keep up the good work. I will continue to seek out the best in all areas of leadership and know that you will have my back when leading.

This is an ongoing practice and learning opportunity. We must stand together to inspire the next generation to be successful leaders. Enjoy all your leadership opportunities and remember to grow in your leadership and provide solutions that impact others.

LEADERSHIP SCORE CARD

This 28 Question Score Card will give you an understanding of your leadership skills and show how to improve your leadership role. "Add the numbers together to know your leadership rank"

1. **Do you enjoy leading?**

   1 2 3 4 5 6 7 8 9 10

2. **Does your leadership intertwine with work or your occupation.**

   1 2 3 4 5 6 7 8 9 10

3. **Do you lead or follow in your children's activities, school plays, school sports, church events etc.**

   1 2 3 4 5 6 7 8 9 10

4. **Did you lead or follow as a child, including your teenage years?**

   1 2 3 4 5 6 7 8 9 10

5. **Do you enjoy following rather than leading?**

   1 2 3 4 5 6 7 8 9 10

6. **Are you a leader in the community?**

   1 2 3 4 5 6 7 8 9 10

7. **Do you have leadership skills?**

   1 2 3 4 5 6 7 8 9 10

8. **Can you lead a team of five without doubt?**

   1 2 3 4 5 6 7 8 9 10

9. **Do you have an educational degree in leadership?**

    1 2 3 4 5 6 7 8 9 10

10. **Do you lead employment projects or as a self-employed individual business?**

    1 2 3 4 5 6 7 8 9 10

11. **Do you lead church functions or uphold leadership roles?**

    1 2 3 4 5 6 7 8 9 10

12. **Can you lead a diverse team of individuals?**

    1 2 3 4 5 6 7 8 9 10

13. **Are you willing to travel for a leadership role, conference, events, retreats etc.**

    1 2 3 4 5 6 7 8 9 10

14. **Do you engage in events, functions, projects annually?**

    1 2 3 4 5 6 7 8 9 10

15. **Have you lead ever?**

    1 2 3 4 5 6 7 8 9 10

16. **Does leadership help with your ability to understand others?**

    1 2 3 4 5 6 7 8 9 10

17. **Can you learn to lead or become a leader?**

    1 2 3 4 5 6 7 8 9 10

18. **Will your leadership skills help others succeed?**

    1 2 3 4 5 6 7 8 9 10

19. **Does your family lead to greater outcome, family camping, family reunions, family activities or other family events?**

    1 2 3 4 5 6 7 8 9 10

20. **Can you teach someone about leadership?**

    1 2 3 4 5 6 7 8 9 10

21. **Are you involved in service clubs, Rotary, Lions, or any other form of community clubs?**

    1 2 3 4 5 6 7 8 9 10

22. **When leading, did you have good outcomes?**

    1 2 3 4 5 6 7 8 9 10

23. **Can you be a good leader in bad situations?**

1 2 3 4 5 6 7 8 9 10

24. **Do your leadership skills improve or impact on the community?**

1 2 3 4 5 6 7 8 9 10

25. **Are your leadership skills recognized?**

1 2 3 4 5 6 7 8 9 10

26. **Does your physical ability stop you from leading?**

1 2 3 4 5 6 7 8 9 10

27. **Are you a multitask Leader?**

1 2 3 4 5 6 7 8 9 10

28. **You rather be a follower than a leader?**

1 2 3 4 5 6 7 8 9 10

SCORECARD RESULTS

Score Rank 28-69

This indicates that you›re more of a follower than a leader. You're interested in volunteering, leading, or following but, don't. The score means you need to be more active in school, community and volunteerism or be more interested in motivational activities that interest you. You would rather be doing something else than leading or following. You enjoy being in groups and like to apply your skills elsewhere.

Score Rank 70-100

This score suggests room for improvement in your leadership or following skills. You have the skills and the motivation to lead or follow, but you must apply yourself fully. To enhance your skills, you must show more interest in leading or following, not just when it's obligated, but as a proactive choice. You only volunteer for credit or when it's required. Leading is not one of your favorite opportunities. You're interested but need to commit fully, but you can lead when you turn it on.

Score Rank 101-165

This score indicates that your leadership or following skills have been effective. Your active participation in annual events or functions keeps you motivated. You have developed your leadership skills and enjoy leading, which is a significant achievement. You can be a great leader and encourage others in leading roles. Being active and continuing to learn about ethics and leadership theories will help your leadership skills develop. You're devoted but have not fully committed to a full-time leadership role.

Score Rank166-210

This indicates that you're a leader in the community. You address the needs of other leaders and support positive and cultural awareness. The score means you're active in leading and participating in annual events, functions, social gatherings, non-profits, and service groupings. You're also active in learning about leadership and relaying how to be a good leader/follower. Your skills are at their best, and you're leading well. You also uphold leading roles in the community. You're a leader, not a follower.

Score Rank 211-280

This indicates that your occupation or career leads in the community or how our society functions. Your ranking is teacher/principal, policeman, politician, director, nurse/ doctor, CEO, and any other professional position. This score means you're well educated in leadership or have some knowledge of studies. You're a leader and not a follower, which provides opportunities for growth in the community. Your role is ongoing, and you seek out opportunities to lead. You're a great example of good leadership.

REFERENCES

Aragaki, A. (2016, March 31). Small-group decision making. Medium. https://medium.com/@arianaragaki/small-group-decision-making-1549d3017550#:~:text=In%20group%20decision%20making%2C%20there%20are%20four%20different%20phases%20according,are%20about%20to%20deal%20with.

Association, N. E. (n.d.). Code of ethics for educators. NEA. https://www.nea.org/resource-library/code-ethics-educators

Cambridge dictionary: Find definitions, meanings & translations. Cambridge Dictionary: Find Definitions, Meanings & Translations. (n.d.). Retrieved March 11, 2023, from https://dictionary.cambridge.org/us/

Clark, D. (n.d.). Team leadership model. Retrieved August 23, 2022, from http://www.nwlink.com/~donclark/leader/team_leadership.html

Cornell, D., & Drew, C. (2024, January 3). 15 ethical behavior examples. Helpful Professor. https://helpfulprofessor.com/ethical-behavior-examples/

DiFranza, A. (2022, March 19). Transformational leadership: How to inspire innovation in the Workplace. Northeastern University Graduate Programs. Retrieved September 5, 2022, from https://www.northeastern.edu/graduate/blog/transformational

Diversity and inclusive teaching. Center for Teaching and Assessment of Learning. (n.d.). Retrieved August 19, 2022, from https://ctal.udel.edu/resources-2/inclusive-teaching/#:~:text=Teaching%20for%20diversity%20refers%20to,handled%20with%20fairness%20and%20justice.

Diversity and inclusion definitions. Ferris State University. (n.d.). Retrieved August 19, 2022, from https://www.ferris.edu/administration/president/DiversityOffice/Definitions.htm

Diversity competency - University of Delaware. (n.d.). Retrieved August 20, 2022, from https://www.csd.udel.edu/content-sub-site/Documents/CSD%20factsheet%20DC%20-%20framed.pdf

Diversity, equity & in University American Association of Colleges for Teacher Education (AACTE). (2022, May 10). Retrieved August 19, 2022, from https://aacte.org/resources/dei/

Donoghue, K. (2017, August 2). Why did the boys in blue turn into the boys in black? (part 3). Donoghue Solicitors. https://www.donoghue-solicitors.co.uk/boys-in-blue-part-3/

Editorial, K. (n.d.). Code of ethics: Meaning, types, steps, Principles & Example: Keka. Keka HR. https://www.keka.com/code-of-ethics

Fisher's model – small group communication. Communication Theory. (2023, October 15). https://www.communicationtheory.org/fishers-model-small-group-communication/

Glossary of leadership definitions. (n.d.). http://www.nwlink.com/~donclark/leader/leaddef.html

Harris, M. (2017, March 13). The tenets of educational technology leadership: The full series. The International EdTech Blog with Matt Harris Ed.D. https://mattharrisedd.com/2017/04/11/tenets/

Home: Human resources. Chicago State University. (n.d.). Retrieved August 21, 2022, from https://www.csu.edu/humanresources/empdev/

How do transformational leaders inspire and motivate followers? Verywell Mind. Retrieved September 5, 2022, from https://www.verywellmind.com/what-is-transformational-leadership-2795313

How thinking bigger can help your startup achieve greater things. FasterCapital. (n.d.). https://fastercapital.com/content/How-Thinking-Bigger-Can-Help-Your-Startup-Achieve-Greater-Things.html

Labrecque, K. (n.d.). What authentic leadership is and why showing up as yourself matters. What Authentic Leadership Is and Why Showing Up As Yourself Matters. Retrieved August 20, 2022, from https://www.betterup.com/blog/authentic-leadership#:~:text=%E2%80%9CAuthentic%20leadership%20is%20a%20style,making%20room%20for%20others%2C%20too.

Lee, S. (2022, July 27). 10 leadership styles and their pros and cons. Torch. Retrieved September 5, 2022, from https://torch.io/blog/10-leadership-styles-and-their-pros-and-cons/

Maheshwari, H. (2020, May 13). Covid-19: Finance leadership framework to establish Long Term Financial and operational resilience. LinkedIn. https://www.linkedin.com/pulse/covid-19-framework-establish-long-term-financial-harish-maheshwari/

Mattone, J., & Murray, M. B. (2019). The intelligent leader: Unlocking the 7 secrets to leading others and leaving your legacy. Gildan Media.

McMaster, J. (2013). Common sense leaders. Retrieved August 21, 2022, from http://www.commonsenseleaders.com/summariesandreviews/what-is-team-leadership/

Neale, P. (2022, July 23). Self-reflection in leadership – part 1: Ambitions, values, and personality. Unabridged Leadership. Retrieved August 29, 2022, from https://unabridgedleadership.com/self-reflection-in-leadership/#:~:text=Self%2Dreflection%20in%20leadership%20means,you%20seek%20to%20influence%20others.

Oliver, D. E., & Hioco, B. (2012). An Ethical Decision-Making Framework for Community College Administrators. Community College Review, 40(3), 240-254. https://doi.org/10.1177/0091552112445611

Rosencrance, L. (2021, March 2). What are diversity, Equity, and Inclusion (Dei)? SearchHRSoftware. Retrieved August 19, 2022, from https://www.techtarget.com/searchhrsoftware/definition/diversity-equity-and-inclusion-DEI

Ruíz-Cano, J., Cantú-Quintanilla, G. R., Ávila-Montiel, D., Gamboa-Marrufo, J. D., Juárez-Villegas, L. E., de Hoyos-Bermea, A., Chávez-López, A., Estrada-Ramírez, K. P., Merelo-Arias, C. A., Altamirano-Bustamante, M. M., de la Vega-Morell, N., Peláez-Ballestas, I., Guadarrama-Orozco, J. H., Muñoz-Hernández, O., & Garduño-Espinosa, J. (2015a, March 1). Review of models for the analysis of ethical dilemmas. Boletín Médico del Hospital Infantil de México (English Edition). https://www.elsevier.es/es-revista-boletin-medico-del-hospital-infantil-201-articulo-review-models-for-analysis-ethical-X2444340915346044#:~:text=SAD%20Formula,well%20as%20the%20solutions%20adopted.

Semczuk, N. (2019, April 30). 5 lifelong lessons from the magic of thinking big by David Schwartz. Medium. https://medium.com/@nina.semczuk/5-lifelong-lessons-from-the-magic-of-thinking-big-by-david-schwartz-6b33f5b21fae

Slideshare. (2014, August 13). THE SAD FORMULA. SlideShare. https://www.slideshare.net/robintgreene/59185-06p-37975179

Skulmowski, A. (n.d.). Ethical issues of educational virtual reality. https://doi.org/10.1016/j.cexr.2023.100023

Team, P. F. (2024, January 26). Mastering Time Management for Finance Professionals: TIPS and Benefits. https://www.peakframeworks.com/post/time-management

The Evolution of Leadership Theories: From Great Man to Situational Leadership. The Economic Times. (2023).

The Mind Tools Content Team by the Mind Tools Content Team, Team, Gibbs' reflective cycle. Helping People Learn from Experience. Retrieved August 29, 2022, from Western Governors University. (2020, April 27). What is authentic leadership? Western Governors University. Retrieved August 20, 2022, from https://www.wgu.edu/blog/what-is-authentic-leadership2004.html

https://www.mindtools.com/pages/article/reflective-cycle.htm

Turley, R. (2023, June 13). What is ethical leadership in education?. Educational Leadership Degree. https://www.educationalleadershipdegree.com/frequently-asked-questions/what-is-ethical-leadership-in-education/

Wells, S., & Herie, M. (2018). Reflective leadership practice for academic chairs. The Department Chair, 29(1), 1–3. https://doi.org/10.1002/dch.30196

Western Governors University. (2020, April 27). What is authentic leadership? Western Governors University. Retrieved August 20, 2022, from https://www.wgu.edu/blog/what-is-authentic-leadership2004.html

What is the difference between a leader and a manager? NSLS. (n.d.). https://www.nsls.org/blog/what-is-the-difference-between-a-leader-and-a-manager

Winn, M. (2013, June 15). The power of thinking big - the view inside me. The View Inside Me - The World Changing Blog by Marc Winn. https://theviewinside.me/the-power-of-thinking-big/

Wizbowski, R. (n.d.). Ethical leadership: Fostering a culture of integrity from the top down. Diligent. https://www.diligent.com/resources/blog/ethical-leadership

Writer, J. S. (2022, July 14). Leader vs manager: Key traits to adopt. Jobberman Nigeria. https://www.jobberman.com/discover/leader-vs-manager

Zaleznik, A. (2024, February 16). Managers and leaders: Are they different? Harvard Business Review. https://hbr.org/2004/01/managers-and-leaders-are-they-different

Zhang, Y., Adams, D., Cheah, K.S.L. (2023). Technology Leadership for Schools in the Twenty-First Century. In: Adams, D. (eds) Educational Leadership. Springer, Singapore. https://doi.org/10.1007/978-981-99-8494-7_10

Printed in the United States
by Baker & Taylor Publisher Services